Dear Young Nigerian

THE AWAKENING

OGBOLE AGALA

DEAR YOUNG NIGERIAN:

THE AWAKENING

OGBOLE AGALA

PROPAGATE
Publishing

Published in Nigeria by Propagate Publishing
+2348051186514

Cover Photo: Shot by Emmanuel 'Lecoles' Abor
Cover Dessign: Philip Sughnen Gbir-Agera

To the memory of OGBENU G'IDU JOHN AGALA, my father, on whose shoulders I stand tall.

To my Family, the greatest gift I have.

To the memory of Nigeria's heroes past

.

To every young Nigerian striving selflessly for the emergence of a new Nigeria.

To generations unborn, for whom we work tirelessly to bequeath a Nigeria in which it would be extremely difficult to believe that things were the way they are right now.

Content

Preface

Dear Young Nigerian,

I write to inspire new conversations along lines that are different than those we have always had before now.

In a bid to find solutions to problems that have plagued us and our country for such a long time, we focus much attention on the government. This is exactly why we have made little or no progress with regards to finding the right answers to lingering questions.

At this point, taking a different path is the wisest thing to do; otherwise, we may remain at the same undesirable spot perpetually.

As young Nigerians – home and abroad, we must focus more attention on ourselves to derive solutions to our problems. If we keep doing otherwise, we may have to keep up with the unbearable sufferings we have been facing for a very long time. Our hopes have consistently been dashed by the older generation of leaders in our country. If we do nothing more than all we have done so far, things will only get worse, all to our detriment.

We must brace up to the challenges that confront us, with a firm resolve to refrain from retreating, until we begin to yield the fruits of our labour. We must deliberately take our destinies and that of our country into our hands, and see to it that we rise from the dust and ashes in which we have been plunged. We must ensure we break free from the huge chains that bind us right now.

I have written ten different letters to you, and to myself, in order that we may start conversations that will birth progressive actions. This book of letters is not an end in itself, but a means to an end that we start the kind of conversations I have talked about. I hope that we work together to come up with comprehensive blueprints that reflect both short and long term strategies with which we must change the trajectory of our story, by deliberately disturbing the peace of stale and undesirable status quo.

A great Awakening is upon us, let THE CONVERSATION begin!

-Ogbole Agala.
2018.

THE PLEDGE

Dear Young Nigerian,

We do not need to look too far to learn how to be patriotic citizens of our country Nigeria. All we need do is strive deliberately to actualize the provisions of our national pledge.

While in nursery school, young Nigerians are made to recite the national pledge, especially at school functions. This happens up until secondary school. Thereafter, we rarely encounter occasions where it is mandatory to recite the pledge.

Have you ever taken out time to meditate on the provisions of the Nigerian National Pledge?

No doubt, students are compelled to memorize it while in nursery, primary and secondary schools. They do so for fear of what may happen at assembly grounds if one fails to recite it correctly. This is a major reason why we hardly pause to ponder on the words contained therein; hence the difficulty in putting them to practice.

I think it is expedient that I attempt a detailed contextual explanation of the words that make up our national pledge, so we could learn of what they truly mean. Once we have sufficient understanding, we could witness positive changes on account of new attitudes and actions sourced therefrom.

I:

The "I" here refers to you and me as individuals. It refers to every Nigerian distinctly, signifying that every one of us is personally responsible for actualizing the provisions of the pledge. We ought to carry this out as a civic duty, as well as a moral responsibility. Think deeply about this.

...pledge:

A pledge is a binding commitment to do, or refrain from doing certain things, in honour of a person, thing or entity. When we make a pledge to Nigeria, it is a solemn promise, undertaking, vow, commitment, bond, oath and guarantee to carry out all the responsibilities outlined in the pledge.

We are individually and collectively bound by our words, haven promised to be faithful, loyal and honest; to serve Nigeria with all our strength, to defend her unity and uphold her honour and glory.

Just like I have said earlier, it is like any other oath, which must be kept – in the interest of the person making it. Breaking an oath usually has consequences. In the case of breaking our pledge to Nigeria, we may not necessarily be visited with legal sanctions per se. However, we can trace the undesirable state of affairs in our country the breach of our national pledge on diverse fronts by most of us. If only we did those things contained in our pledge, such undesirable state of affairs could be remedied, mitigated or even avoided. Could it be that the circumstances on ground right now would have been a lot better if there were clear sanctions prescribed by law; specifically for violating the oath taken while reciting the national pledge? We ought not to wait till it gets to that point before we do what is right.

...to Nigeria my country

This part of our pledge portrays Nigeria as something personal to each and every one of us. It means Nigeria is yours personally, as well as mine too. Naturally, there is a good way we treat things that are ours, especially if those things are of great value. Most of us hardly treat Nigeria this way. There is this atmosphere around us that makes it seem as if although we are Nigerians, the country may not necessarily be ours. This is so because for so many years, prevailing circumstances have engraved certain negative images on our minds, consequent upon which we cede all that should be ours to those who benefit selfishly from the system.

We may be tempted to care less about Nigeria, as a result of undesirable circumstances. You hear many of us make statements like "I am not interested in politics" "Na them sabi" "wetin concern me" etc. We fail to understand that whatever happens at the socio-political and economic arena affects us all, one way or another. Most of us exhibit this attitude, thereby giving room for our country to be swayed by just a few persons who are obsessed with being in control of everything from top to bottom.

Sometimes, we compare Nigeria with other countries, spotting things that go on well in those countries which we do not see in ours. We go as far as referring to foreign nations as "saner climes", invariably meaning our clime is otherwise. It is sad that we hardly sit back to really think about those factors that may be responsible in other countries for the good things we wish were obtainable in ours.

We must realize that the good systems and things in other countries are products of deliberate efforts made by citizens who regard their country as theirs personally and collectively in every sense; citizens who are sincerely willing to do whatever it takes to make contributions to positive developments and advancements, as much as it lies within their power. We cannot continue to treat Nigeria with levity and attitudes that portray indifference or insensitivity, and expect her to advance in desired positive directions.

The major problem here is that we sustain an erroneous mindset that vests the responsibility of making this country work solely on the government, without accepting and working on our own part of the shared responsibility.

No doubt, the government and all institutions of the state at all levels have very huge roles to play, but as citizens, we also have as much roles to play too. We cannot expect any positive results when we keep pushing our own part of the responsibilities to the government – which has been unable to handle its own part satisfactorily.

No country can experience positive growth and advancement without the deliberate and active participation of patriotic citizens. The foundation of patriotism can only be laid once we begin to regard Nigeria as ours; when she becomes of great value to most of us who are citizens. The path towards achieving this is a deliberate one. It should be taken against all odds; and in spite of circumstances that project discouragements.

...to be faithful, loyal and honest

If we desire to live in a country we are proud of, faithfulness, loyalty and honesty are virtues we cannot do without. They must be perpetually woven into the fabric of our lives and expressed in every bit of our daily interactions.

Unfortunately, these virtues have become endangered species in our territory, such that – more often than not, a person who exhibits even the slightest trait of faithfulness, loyalty or honesty, is regarded as a strange human, or even a fool. This ought not to be so.

Now, what does it really mean to be faithful?

What are the attributes through which we can distinguish between someone who is faithful and one who is not? We need to understand this sufficiently in order to live it out.

Faithfulness entails unwavering fidelity. It is the quality of being steadfast in affection or allegiance, and being constant, true, devoted, dedicated, and committed.

Although a few exist, it is difficult to find many young Nigerians who sincerely owe allegiance to Nigeria, and manifest such allegiance by selflessly pursuing causes aimed at moving our country forward. We ought to sustain a disposition of faithfulness, if we expect to make any meaningful advancement beyond our current position.

What does it mean to be loyal?

To be loyal in this context is to have an unwavering devotion, which is inspired and sustained by love for our country. A loyal Nigerian is one who engages in giving and showing firm and constant support for Nigeria; one who is devoid of any unhealthy bias or unreasonable sentimental attachments that promote selfish interests. Can we really say we love our country – especially selflessly? Without this love for Nigeria, we cannot be loyal to her. This is because loyalty is always tested, and it definitely fails where genuine, selfless and fervent love is absent.

From the negative comments most of us make concerning Nigeria, and the bad light in which we portray her on a daily basis, it is obvious we do not even love our country in the first place, let alone sustain the desire to be loyal, notwithstanding the negative circumstances around us.

We may say our negative outlooks and remarks about our country are justified by the undesirable circumstances in which we find ourselves today, but it is so sad that most of us only stop at the point of identifying and analyzing problems. We heap blames on everyone else but ourselves, without thinking of practical solutions to these problems. This is why we move round endless cycles, making little or no reasonable headway towards sustainable growth and development on all fronts.

I am of the opinion that it all ends in futility if we are able to identify and vocalize problems without proffering feasible and pragmatic solutions to such problems at the end of the day. If you identify a problem, the first thing you ought to do is sit down and think of workable solutions before you begin to vocalize such a problem. A reasonable rant should end with objective recommendations that have the capacity to solve identified problems.

Now, let us talk about honesty.

To be honest is to be frank and indisposed to deception, cheating and fraud. Someone who is honest is truthful, sincere, straightforward, and free of deceit.

We see how much this virtue is lacking as we interact with the systems in place and with each other on individual and group levels. In fact, being suspicious of one another has become instinctive. Our initial disposition when we interact is to be doubtful of the candidness behind each other's motives. We sustain the same disposition when interacting with the systems in place, and the country by extension.

Why is this so? Many of us are not honest in our dealings with others because of the gains we seek to obtain through fraudulent means. In fact, sometimes, we are dishonest to ourselves, playing to the galleries whenever we perceive the availability of some form of advantage, even if it may be detrimental to other people and to our country at large.

The insufficient level of honesty is a major factor responsible for our inability to band together and make concerted efforts towards advancing our country and making it a better place for all of us and for posterity. We need to do things differently in this regard. Our society would be a lot better if we deal with each other honestly. We must do this both as a civic duty and a moral responsibility, if we intend to drive Nigeria through a steadily progressive path.

...to serve Nigeria with all my strength

To serve is to carry out a function or play a role in order to actualize a purpose. A person who serves is one who is of use in achieving a goal.

Serving Nigeria entails carrying out positive actions deliberately, in order to promote the country's interests along developmental lines. We can serve Nigeria in so many ways. It starts with sustaining a patriotic disposition, such that is anchored on sincere love for our country. This is the bedrock upon which any form of service can make reasonable contributions that may be of benefit to our commonwealth. While we sustain a patriotic state of mind, we must let it influence our daily interactions with the systems in place, and also with other people and groups, so as to successfully propagate the message of patriotism.

How exactly can we be patriotic? When we prioritize the interest of our country over and above selfish interests, and deliberately pursue those things that advance her growth and development, we are being patriotic. Patriots do not take things for granted when it has to do with their country. This can be clearly seen in the way they go about their daily activities, as well as the interactions they engage in.

Patriotism or the lack of it also reflects specifically in the way people go about their work. To be patriotic, those who work in the public sector must carry out their responsibilities in such a way that shows they have the interest of this country at heart, and not just their selfish interests. They must be willing to promote Nigeria's advancement on all positive fronts, starting from their immediate spheres of influence. Whatever stands in the way of such service must be disregarded, no matter the consequences. Nigeria must come first, over and above anyone's selfish interest. This can only be achieved through deliberate endeavours.

Service to the nation is not restricted to those who work in public offices. Private sector employees ought to also serve Nigeria by carrying out their responsibilities with the interests of the nation at heart. This should be manifest in how they treat people, their attitude towards work, integrity, etc.

If you are a young Nigerians who is still a student, you are not left out. You should also sustain a patriotic state of mind, with the willingness to serve Nigeria and promote her interests always. For young Nigerians in the diaspora, you ought to conduct yourselves in ways that project a positive image of Nigeria. We are acquainted with the negative light in which our country has been painted before the world on account of the misdeeds of a few individuals. We must strive to generate a narrative that is otherwise, by upholding the values prescribed by our national pledge, notwithstanding whether we are at home or abroad. We should also strive earnestly to ensure excellence is aimed at and achieved in all of our endeavours.

In all, we serve Nigeria by doing all we ought to do in pursuit of her interests over selfish ones. As we do so, we must also encourage others to do same, by enlightening them on the benefits of service to our country and the consequences of neglecting such vital service.

We must note that the line of our pledge that talks of service specifically states how such service should be carried out. It states: *"...with all my strength."* This means that service to Nigeria must be done with the whole quantity or extent of our strength. It is not to be done lackadaisically, lazily or grudgingly; but with such force and determination to see something good result from our individual and collective efforts. This is why reasonable service can only be done consciously, by those who have the clear goal of promoting Nigeria's interests at heart.

...to defend her unity

Now, this is a sensitive part of our pledge which we ought to consider very carefully. First, we must understand what it really means to defend a thing. It simply means to protect it from harm or attacks. To defend is to resist an attack or safeguard something or someone from harm or danger.

A defender works to ensure that whatever threatens the object of his or her defense is properly dealt with and prevented from carrying out such threats.

By virtue of the provisions of our national pledge, the object of our defense is Nigeria's unity. We can define unity as the state of being joined as a whole. Unity is at the instance of integration, on account of which a complete and harmonious whole is formed, without any form of strife or discord that threatens its continuity.

The unity of Nigeria refers to such territorial oneness that is unbroken by any factor whatsoever that may seek to split the country into two or more independent entities. It also refers to the harmonious coexistence of individuals and groups from divergent backgrounds, who may subscribe to different beliefs, ideologies or cultures.

You and I are either witnesses or accomplices to the unhealthy magnification of our diversity by agents who seek to generate more reasons why the territorial entity called Nigeria should cease to exist in one piece.

We complain – sometimes rightly so, of diverse forms of "marginalization" on account of which people in some sections of the country enjoy more privileges and advantages than others.

The Federal Character Principle was set in place to guard against such marginalization. It prescribes equal representation of people from each part of the country at the national level, whenever and wherever there is provision for such.

We can say that several agitations and actions geared towards splitting the country up are inspired by both real and imagined violations of the standard of equality prescribed by the Federal Character Principle; and other specific legal provisions against any form of discrimination or undue advantage or disadvantage which is linked to our diversity.

If we read in-between the lines objectively and in all sincerity, we would realize that beyond any actual undoing that triggers dissatisfaction and consequent agitations along this line, we are prone to being influenced by group or personal biases, sentiments or insecurities, when looking into issues that bother on those factors that seek to divide us.

Can we ponder on what Nigeria would be like if we all tried to look beyond our selfish interests, and work together to sustain a unified country? Believe it or not, we all need each other. Each part of the country compliments the others in ways that make it more desirable to continue as a single entity – strongly bonded together, irrespective of our differences. In fact, our beauty lays in the diversity every person or group is able to bring to the table of unity.

We cannot overlook or overemphasize this issue of unity, as it is most sacrosanct to our advancement. It breeds peace, without which there can be no meaningful development.

As young Nigerians, we must do as much as lies within our power to defend the unity of Nigeria. We cannot afford to bequeath a battered and fragmented country to those who will come after us. We must shun, expose and run down those wicked men and women who try to toy with our senses by stimulating, bloating and propagating biases. Their ultimate aim is to exploit the outcomes of the schemes they orchestrate, to their advantage and to our detriment.

...and uphold her honour and glory

In this context, to uphold means to maintain, preserve or protect. Honour means high respect and great esteem. Glory means prestige, acclamation, or high renown won by notable achievements.

Putting these together, it is clear that we ought to maintain, preserve and protect the high respect, great esteem, prestige, acclamation and high renown of Nigeria; which was achieved by the notable accomplishments of our heroes past, and which is being achieved by those who work tirelessly today to yield honour and glory for our country. We must be deliberate about this and refrain from treating it lightly. As young Nigerians, we should work tirelessly to replicate or improve on those things that generate honour and glory. Delivering excellence in our various fields of endeavor could take us to points where our country is honoured around the world because of us.

Technological and social innovation, community development, capacity building and diverse forms of advocacies will go a long way to generate honourable and glorious outcomes, if done with diligence, sufficient knowledge and skills. When the opposite is the case, the outcome will be an erosion of the honour and glory we already have. Also, there will be little or no chances of actualizing new feats along this line, both individually and collectively.

The name "Nigeria" rings a bell with diverse sounds around the world. Some sounds are for positive reasons, while others are for negative reasons. All of these are on account of how the world regards us, judging from our actions or omissions. Our friends in the diaspora have a great role to play in changing the negative narratives about us, and portraying Nigeria in positive light, before the international community. Those back home equally have a great role to play, pursuant to the restoration, sustenance and advancement of our honour and glory.

We need to get things right by our deliberate actions. This should not just be in a bid to have a positive image before the rest of the world, but also for the enormous benefits that are bound to fall upon us and our country in the process.

...so help me God.

After all is said and done, we still need God's help to fulfill our pledge to Nigeria. There is no guarantee that the paths towards fulfilling our oath would be a smooth one. We will surely have to encounter hurdles, especially as we wage war against established systems and persons that seek to generate and perpetuate circumstances that make it difficult for us to fulfill our pledge to Nigeria.

We must pray to receive God's help to enable us achieve those things we are incapable of achieving all by ourselves. While we seek divine help, we must not fail to play our own part diligently.

Think about these things deeply.

Let THE CONVERSATION begin.

Yours,

Ogbole Agala.

Second Letter

CABAL SCRIPTS

Dear Young Nigerian,

Allow me point out a certain evil responsible – in no small measure – for the setbacks to Nigeria's advancement. If you are already aware of it, my communication will be some sort of confirmation; whereas if you are unaware, your path to discovery may be lit henceforth.

The major enemies of Nigeria are the so called "Cabals".

I hope this sinks deep down our minds, till we gain perfect understanding of the fact that the rat races we run every day are contents of scripts carefully written and supervised by them. Cabal unions are usually comprised of a handful of inordinately ambitious persons, whose principal aim is to have Nigeria on their palms, to do with her as they please; benefitting enormously therefrom. They employ unimaginable physical, mental and diabolic means to achieve their aims. The successful perpetuation of each of their scheme is sustained by the gullibility of their victims. Such gullibility flourishes on a very high level of induced ignorance, which stems from continuous deception and carefully calculated plans to shroud weighty matters, while presenting trivialities to the masses on daily basis.

The Cabal works so hard through their agents to distract and keep Nigerians busy, while they go about the business of doing and undoing graver stuffs, in a bid to determine the path through which Nigeria navigates. At their instance, we have been on a wrong trajectory for so long.

It is difficult to see all of these, simply because cabals purpose that Nigerians remain blinded from realities. Their activities are carried out in the dark, making it impossible for people outside their folds to have the slightest glimpse into what they are really up to.

Young Nigerians must understand that at different levels, these evil networks are comprised of far more dangerous personalities than we think we know already. Their well-organized structures incorporate few members from different parts of Nigeria.

Far beyond what meets the eye, their operations are not hindered by tribal, religious, economic or political differences. They are united in the dark, to the detriment of the rest of us who are victims of their lethal orchestrations.

We need to understand that notwithstanding the things we may see, there is a huge difference between the actual problems of Nigeria and the superficial concerns cabals deliberately set before our eyes.

They seek to control things from behind the scenes at each level of government in our country. While we are busy acting out their scripts, they buy enough time to make more deadly arrangements that will enable them have a firmer grip on us and our country.

It is sad that the average Nigerian hardly weighs issues with due diligence by asking reasonable and independently thought-out questions about what goes on in this country? More often than not, most of the few persons who ask seemingly reasonable questions do so after weighing issues on biased and sentimental scales. Objectivity is hard to come by. This is all part of cabal scripts we are made to act out unconsciously, on consistent basis. Their schemes tickle our biases and sentiments, thereby further dividing us.

We hardly ever pause to ponder why we take certain actions we would not ordinarily take in our natural state. It is indeed baffling how we arrive at unjustifiable conclusions on issues. Have you ever wondered why exactly you should hate your neighbor as a result of religious, ethnic, political, social or economic differences? It is unnatural. Cabals benefit from the fallouts of our hatred and disunity.

There are pockets of violence every now and then in Nigeria because cabals fuel religious, ethnic and political tensions. We end up acting out their scripts by setting ourselves on fire against each other, to their amusement and unquantifiable benefit. This ought not to be so.

It is no longer surprising that more often than not, breaking news and other media reports end up instigating and sustaining fear, tension, violence, and other undesirable atmospheres. This too, is at the core of cabal scripts.

Young Nigerians must understand that the root cause of every physical or social challenge we face in our country is manmade. It is usually at the instance of a fine blend of cabal activities and our ignorance or gullibility. From this point of understanding, we can begin to make reasonable progress by seeking sufficient knowledge on how to go about tackling the sources of our problems.

It is not like a good number of Nigerians are unaware of these things. A whole lot of us either take these things for granted or fear the perceived consequences of taking the right actions, especially against so called "powers that be." This too is within the purview of the cabal's projections. We ought not to remain this way. It is high time we freed ourselves from this bondage.

One way we can do this is by participating actively in politics, and demanding answers to lingering questions from relevant authorities. This way, it will be difficult for cabals to keep us in the dark via their minions in office.

Cabals control wealth, and so they can make a good number of people poor and also buyable when the need arises. This is why so much poverty ravages the land at some point in time, only for plenty of money to exchange hands during elections or whenever "big men" need one form of support or another from us. They know very well that hungry men are likely to be bought over to carry out the wishes of their buyers, provided they can eat at last. We need to renew our minds to detest such, and teach others to do same.

It is so sad that social media platforms help cabals keep Nigerians (especially young people) distracted. Each new day offers brand new issues which become objects of rants, forcing us to discard what we started talking about just yesterday. The things that happen around us are carefully arranged, and spread through the media. In the end, we are kept occupied as usual. These people play with our senses; most times successfully.

Once a thing tickles or pinches our sentiments, many of us consider and pay so much attention to whatever anybody opens his or her mouth to say. Most times, it is not necessarily because of the particular things said (which we may not even try to understand before arguing or fighting around or about), but because of our long-lived suspicion of each other, which has become instinctive. Cabals know and exploit this avenue, since they have vast experience when it comes to operating the buttons that make us kill each other in compliance with the scripts they author. We need to be freed from their chains, especially mentally.

To break free, we need to imbibe the culture of persistency, by virtue of which we continuously stay on matters, demanding answers to questions and reemphasizing our desires till they are brought into fruition by relevant stakeholders, no matter how long it takes.

I have written all of the forgoing to the end that young Nigerians would see things clearly for what they are, and deliberately begin to think and act differently than how we have always done. We must begin to weigh matters and reason independently, avoiding the practice of swallowing hook, line and sinker whatever cabals force down our throats. The era of biased and sentimental adoption of whatever we are made to perceive is over. We must break off the shackles with which cabals bind us to the ground.

We must deliberately and diligently perform the role of manning the gates of our minds; resisting all forms of manipulation. Once we refuse to act their script, we render them powerless. This is exactly how to run our enemies out of business, and take back this great country which rightfully belongs to us. We must take this path to freedom, damning all consequences. We must refrain from listening to them and doing what they say.

We must generate more ideas on how to run their enterprise to the ground, in such a way it can never be rebuilt.

Think about these things deeply.

Let THE CONVERSATION begin.

Yours,

Ogbole Agala.

<u>Third Letter</u>

DO NOT BE DECEIVED

Dear young Nigerian,

It is no news that the consciences of many among the current crop of politicians are dead. Why hail or wail over these people, when you are being dragged into a coffin they seek in unison to nail permanently?

I admonish you not to be misled by the seeming sight of divergent camps in their midst. The lines dividing them are only visible from the galleries where we sit. The closer you get to the arena, the less obvious those lines become, till they fade into thin air, disappearing before your eyes, since they were never in existence in the first place. If by any means you stand in their midst, you will not miss the realization that the lines in question are only figments of our imaginations; and not part of their reality. They are bound together by such a strong chord that functions to their profit, and to the detriment of those of us outside their cliques. What is at stake is of more importance to them than their differences, so they bond, beyond our sight.

We work with theories of division which are applicable only to us, and not to those who brew wine off our sweat and blood, getting drunk thereby. This ought not to be.

Taking into cognizance contemporary happenings within the political sphere in Nigeria, could there be a better time than this for young Nigerians to put on their thinking caps?

I think not. Now is the time to do this, and we must do it quick, otherwise, we may remain lost. Does anyone need celestial abilities to understand that whatever drives the cabals – and their foot soldiers in places of authority, has no bearing on our collective interests? I want to believe that only the dead may be incapable of such understanding.

One thing is clear from all we have witnessed in the recent past: the game is all about the acquisition and preservation of diverse selfish interests. The insatiable cravings for power, as well as the illicit desire to have unlimited access to the bounties of our commonwealth – at all cost, are responsible for the absurd desperation of cryptic cabals working behind the scenes, and their representatives on stage.

They treat our intelligence with wanton disregard, banking on their antecedents to scheme their ways into such power that enjoys the quality of perpetuity. They rest, assured that they will always have idle minds at their service; people who would feed off illicit provisions and act according to their promptings, mortgaging their conscience and future for coins and bread.

I will tell you a couple of things we ought to do now, to sustain the survival of our country and ensure that the sanity and peaceful existence of well-meaning Nigerians remain intact. This is of utmost importance.

First, our minds must be renewed to accommodate the fact that in this country of ours, the various components of competence, leadership capacity and good governance have little or no bearing on the political party from whence a leader hails. We are witnesses to the fact that it is consistently trendy for politicians to jump from one political party to another, shamelessly going back and forth in search of any platform that could facilitate their agendas. They may give diverse reasons for their actions, while attempting to convince us that our collective interests necessitate their movements. However, you need not think too far to decipher that such tales are only blatant lies, factored into the thread of deceptive devices with which they purpose to keep us perpetually bound in deep pits, with very heavy shackles. The tussle for who handles the scepter of authority is driven by nothing but their selfish interests.

To address this issue, we must learn to separate and identify politicians as individuals who are distinguishable from whatever political party they may belong to.

We must realize that a bad and incompetent leader does not automatically transform into a good and competent one by simply jumping from one political party to another. In a new political party, he or she is more likely to remain bad and incompetent, to say the least.

The lack of concrete political ideologies is responsible for a whole lot of the nonsense that goes on in the realm of political party politics in Nigeria. It is obvious that most of these parties only aim to win elections – by hook and crook, and to cling unto power perpetually. This is why politicians jump here and there at the slightest impulse. This show of shame and absurd desperation must be discouraged.

Come to think of it, if holding a political office is as service oriented as it ought to be in reality, I think we should be begging people to lead us. We would not find such desperation if they had no ulterior motives to milk our commonwealth dry, and enrich themselves to our detriment. If it were really about service to the people the way they make it look, most politicians would have been reluctant to seek our mandate. But as it is right now, all we see is mere deceitful drama. In reality, they do not have our interest at heart.

It is so sad that more often than not, the political party of an aspirant is the major standard with which we measure and decide whether or not to support them. This ought not to be. Henceforth, young Nigerians must approach things differently. We need to ensure that we support or vote based on our convictions regarding the competence of individuals; and not necessarily because of their party affiliations. A monkey will always remain a monkey, notwithstanding the tree on which it abides, or that onto which it jumps. Therefore, an aspirant is not worth our support merely because of his political party ties. His or her individual capacity and competence should be the major determining factor, notwithstanding their political parties. We must grow our democracy to this level if we intend to make any progress beyond the point where we are stuck right now – on account of incompetent leadership.

There is this crippling apprehension of being in the minority. We tend to vote based on who we think is more likely to win an election, and not necessarily because we believe in their leadership abilities and capacity to deliver the dividends of good governance. This ought not to be.

It is better to stand for what you believe and support someone who ends up losing an election, than to ride in a bandwagon, contributing your quota to the emergence of disastrous leaderships.

Do not promote the actualization of the selfish the interests of a select few, against our collective interests as a people.

Desist from fighting your neighbor, and let us band effectively, to wage a decisive war against our actual enemies.

You and I know very well that their children and loved ones are in the arms of safety and abundance, far away from harm's way; and nowhere near the calamities into which their fathers plunge us consistently. Wisdom should speak to us in this regard, furnishing our hearts with the realization that we are of little or no value in the eyes of these people. They regard us as good enough only to serve their selfish interests.

If up until now, you deliberately choose to be blinded by crumbs from their tables – making yourself available to be used as a tool to facilitate the installation and perpetuation of bad leadership, then you are not just your personal problem, but our collective problem. We have to solve you too, like every other problem.

We must persist in doing as much as we can to solve lingering problems. Erasing the memories of cabals and their illicit trade of "godfatherism" should be of paramount interest to us as we work very hard to liberate our country from bondage.

We can successfully achieve this by letting go of our perceived differences. We must seek ways of coming together as young Nigerians at all levels, to pursue the way forward for our country. We cannot rely on the current crop of leaders to take us out of the dark places they have plunged us into all through the years.

We must help ourselves and our country by ourselves.

Think about these things deeply.

Let THE CONVERSATION begin.

Yours,

Ogbole Agala.

<u>*Fourth Letter*</u>
DOUBLE-EDGED SWORDS

Dear Young Nigerian,

Far be it from me that I refrain from expounding certain sensitive matters within the bounds of my knowledge, as much as I have peace within me to communicate them to you. This is notwithstanding the risk of being labeled inappropriately.

Right now, I need to tell you that there are hydra-headed conspiracies against us and our country, at the instance of wicked men, whose schemes are aimed at keeping us in bondage perpetually. The conspiracies I speak of are made effective by a combination of both spiritual and physical forces, harmonized into a double edged sword, used to pierce and cut in pieces those things that should ensure the enjoyment of our livelihood.

The success and perpetuity of the objects of these conspiracies are driven on the wheels of our insufficient knowledge, willful denial or indifference regarding their existence – especially the spiritual aspects.

There is a whole lot cabals and their subservient politicians do to cling onto power, so as to sustain the wickedness they perpetrate. They engage the services of very sound intellectuals and skilled strategists, to generate schemes in furtherance of their agendas. They forge ahead to implement such schemes, thereby causing setbacks to our development.

It is a very good thing that there is a voracious mental awakening sweeping across the youth population in Nigeria. Many of us have arrived at an understanding that things ought not to be the way they are right now. This understanding should be backed up by a firm resolve to act in ways that will oust both the maggots and the rottenness they have created and plunged us into. We can use this as a weapon to combat the fallouts of the physical and mental aspects of the conspiracies against us.

However, doing this will not suffice to deal with their conspiracies totally, especially considering the spiritual aspects involved. We must tackle spiritual problems spiritually. In line with this, we must realize that physical and mental factors are mere branches on the tree that produces those behaviours that instigate our reference to many Nigerians as gullible. This tree is firmly rooted in the spiritual realm.

The grounds upon which we are prone to reckon division and enmity as natural consequences of our diversity are also of the same form.

There is a spiritual world – beyond our naked eyes, that serves as the foremost influence on things and circumstances that are manifest in our physical world. Whether or not we choose to believe, disbelieve or willfully deny this fact is inconsequential to its reality.

A lot of things go on at night, which are not discernable with physical senses. These wicked men and their agents engage the services of sorcerers, diviners, mediums, star gazers, oracles, demons and all manner of evil conductors to saturate and infest the atmosphere with pollutants that manifest as catastrophes in the day time. People's minds are also influenced to act in ways they will ordinarily not act.

Sadly, we wake up at dawn, trying to use only our minds/intellects, hands and mouths to fight the consequences of the evil perpetrated against us by spiritual means. Things cannot work that way.

Now, this is what we must do: we must engage the use of a double edged sword. One edge would address the physical aspects of our problems through well-informed and calculated actions. The other edge would serve to combat problems that are spiritual in nature.

While we engage in a mental revolution through progressive conversations and physical actions, we must regard spiritual exercises as of utmost importance in the line of activities geared towards turning the tides in which we have been drowning for years in Nigeria. This must be treated as an emergency – with all seriousness, otherwise in the end, we may be wasting our time with any form of mental and physical awakening we try to promote. This is not withstanding how hard we work at it.

I state without mincing words that we must pray! pray!! and pray!!! This should go hand-in-hand with the physical actions we take; otherwise, the full cycle that should oust the evil in which we have been immersed will remain incomplete. We must not fall victim to the current web of deception that seeks to portray prayers and other spiritual activities as useless ventures carried out by bigots, or people who are not "woke."

Also, we must consciously refrain from taking exclusively extreme positions along this line. On the one hand, we should not subscribe to the extreme which regards prayers and other spiritual activities as the only way out. On the other hand, we should not subscribe to the extreme that regards only mental and physical activities as the way out.

Both ends must be fused in one, thus creating a double-edged sword. We must put this double-edged sword into effective use, so as to successfully fight to a standstill, the evil before us that attacks with its own double-edged sword.

In essence, while we mobilize physical actions to tackle the problems we face on account of the physical systems in place, we must also engage spiritual activities to tackle problems that originate spiritually. If we do otherwise, desired and intended outcomes will never be actualized.

Think about these things deeply.

Let THE CONVERSATION begin.

Yours,

Ogbole Agala.

Fifth Letter

SYCOPHANCY

Dear Young Nigerian,

Other than the unthinkable personal wickedness of some politicians and other highly placed individuals, a frontline disaster plaguing our socio-political arena is sycophancy. In fact, it is the very thick veil that blinds the eyes of so many leaders, making it impossible for them to clearly see how that their leadership is nothing but regrettable. Sycophancy disables whatever it takes for leaders to hear the actual cries of the people they lead. It erodes their capacity to feel the actual pains of the masses, since they are fed with thick lies that portray everything as being okay.

You see, a sycophant is a person who tries to please someone else via words or actions, in order to gain personal benefits. He or she tries to win favor from influential people by flattery, worship and other cunning means, at the expense of truth, virtue and self-worth. Sycophants do not care about how their actions or inactions are detrimental to other people, as long as they gain whatsoever they desire from whosoever thy seek it from.

Their mouths drip like adulterated honey when they speak in the presence of someone they think has something to offer, with which they could gratify their selfish desires.

Politicians and other influential people desperately love to surround themselves with sycophants, so they could hear only sweet things very loudly. This is one major reason why they pay deaf ears to the cries of the masses. The songs that permeate the ears of such leaders are too loud, hence they are unable to hear, let alone consider anything else from their people.

You see, despite the ugly state of affairs in our country, minions do not cease to drum all day long for their lords, who dance shamelessly and retire at dusk to drink and get drunk with the sweat of those they regard as common men. They wake up with hangovers at dawn, saying smelly things that subject everyone else to bondage.

How can leaders be acquainted with actual prevailing circumstances, when they create and live with sycophants in exclusive empires where everything appears rosy?

Their attitudes send messages to everyone outside their small covens suggesting that they should lick the dust. Things should not continue this way.

And so the story goes; sycophancy is the oil that greases a wicked man's self-validation and perpetuation of evil. This is exactly why they would rather surround themselves with loyal minions deliberately, than with persons who could tell them the truth. Once they smell a rat in the air around someone who wants to do something different than cheering them on, they quickly do away with such a person, in order to maintain the status quo of their merry go round, to the detriment of the common man.

You see, we are more likely than not to think that the issue of sycophancy has nothing to do with us. It is easy to classify it as a remote activity carried out by people other than us. But for some of us, if we consider things in all sincerity, we may see how our day to day actions and inactions qualify us as big time sycophants. It may not appear so, but in the end, this may well be the case.

Do you lurk around so called "big men" in order to gain some form of benefits, with no thought of telling them the bitter truth, as and at when due? Do you sing their praises even when it is obvious that they have done nothing worthy of such praises? Do you blindly support and validate leaders and their actions, irrespective of their incompetence, lack of foresight and the outright evils they perpetrate?

If your answers to these questions are in the affirmative – even in the slightest form – then you are a sycophant, for all intents and purposes. You constitute a huge part of the problem and can never be a patriot in that state. If you find yourself in such shoes, you must have a change of heart, and do so consciously and promptly.

We must really begin to understand that a person who lacks sufficient understanding of himself and the degree of his worth is made subject to circumstances under which he is treated in demeaning ways. No one with an accurate valuation of his or her worth would stoop so low to lick the feet of another person, in a bid to derive any form of benefits. No one who realizes the essence of life would sacrifice the truth on the altar of selfishness.

Those leaders who surround themselves with sycophants are not as important as they make themselves look. In fact, they get validation for their actions from people who refrain from telling them the truth. In turn, they part with resources and other benefits, in order to maintain such validation.

This is a major factor why corruption thrives unabated. It is capital intensive to maintain sycophants. Under normal circumstances, a politician may not possess all the resources required to pay for sycophantic services. Hence, they embezzle public funds in order to meet up with the high demands heaped on their shoulders.

As young Nigerians, we ought to take some time out to ponder on what the outcomes may be, if we all make up our minds to deprive wicked leaders of the validation we give to them and the evil the perpetrate. Let the truth be told at all times by fearless citizens who care less for illicit gains and selfish advantages offered by wicked people.

If politicians are starved of sycophantic offerings, they would know the truth about what goes on outside the lavish world in which they live. They would wake up to reality and fulfill the purposes for which they occupy positions via our mandate. They would value the worth of so called ordinary men, without whom their empires cannot be run successfully.

A sycophant is a slave in every sense of the word. Such a person needs to be freed mentally and physically too. It is our duty to help such ones by enlightening them properly.

Young Nigerians must break free from questionable traditions; so we could see things clearly.

How exactly can we achieve this?

It starts with renewing our minds so as to discard every factor upon which selfish inclinations thrive. We must bear in mind that it is more beneficial to strive towards attaining feats that benefit the generality of our society, than settling down for those that are exclusively for our benefits.

We must uphold values that promote our wellbeing and that of our beloved country. As we become conscious of the detriments of sycophancy, we must also begin to deliberately enlighten and sensitize other people who may not be aware.

We must firmly establish the fact that great power belongs to us, if only we could realize and use it effectively, instead of subjecting ourselves to very low places on account of sycophancy.

Building the Nigeria of our dreams requires making a whole lot of sacrifices, without which those dreams will remain wishful thinking – incapable of fulfillment. When we become deliberate about these things, we would soon reap the benefits of our labour.

Someday soon, a new Nigeria will be born, free of such insensitive leadership that is powered by sycophancy.

Think about these things deeply.

Let THE CONVERSATION begin.

Yours,

Ogbole Agala.

<u>Sixth Letter</u>

THOSE THINGS THAT DIVIDE US

Dear Young Nigerian,

It is good we share common grounds regarding the wellbeing of our country Nigeria, consequent upon which we strive to ensure her advancement on all positive fronts.

As a matter of fact, there has been too much of talks about Nigeria's problems. In fact, the proliferation of discourses on this subject matter portrays being vocal about our challenges as though it were a mandatory criterion for survival.

No doubt, we cannot begin to solve problems until we have properly identified them. However, such identification alone takes us nowhere. It is high time we focus more on generating well-considered pragmatic solutions, after which we must take necessary actions towards applying them to the problems that challenge us. In line with this, we must begin by correcting the errors birthed at the instance of prejudiced or out rightly false historical narratives.

The promoters of discord in Nigeria rely on the negative energy generated from how Nigerians see each other – as being irreconcilable, on account of the seeds of discord planted by historical narratives and other factors.

I had a sort of nomadic childhood in which I moved from one part of Nigeria to another with my family. In the course of those movements, I made friends with people from di-vergent backgrounds. We could blend perfectly because we were yet to come in contact with the bias that accompanies extreme and exclusive identification with one's tribal or sectional block. As at that time, we had peers in other parts of the country who were brought up in ways that were different than ours.

Now, assuming persons with such different orientations were to give historical accounts of the '90s, we would definitely have had absolutely different versions of Nigerian history pertaining to the same time. Our accounts would have been influenced by perceptions hinged on peculiar orientations, environments, upbringings and prevailing circumstances. I, for one, would have been more inclined to reflect a unified Nigeria in my account. This would have been contrary to the inclinations of people whose experiences were different than mine. We would have painted unique pictures from individual viewpoints.

It is practically impossible to interpret the present-day correctly, without digging deep into antiquity to ascertain those factors responsible for the contemporary shape of things Considering the importance of our history in line with making things work both in present times and posterity, we must make efforts to sufficiently understand past happenings. We cannot move forward without such understanding. Deliberate efforts must be made with open minds, devoid of bias and rigidly held opinions.

If we must have a balanced account of Nigerian history, we must make concerted efforts to assemble and propagate different accounts from all parts of the country; as opposed to sticking to accounts that appeal to our individual favoritisms. This would help us understand and address factors responsible for tribalism, sectionalism, sentimentalism, religious extremism, nepotism, and the likes.

At this point, I will single out religion as a major source of discord in our country.

I was once a member of an online group that was composed of people who subscribe to different religious persuasions. Day by day, there were diverse exchanges between members who tried to promote their religion, portraying it as superior to all others. The way they went about it made me really sad. In order to maintain my sanity, I had to exit the group. But before I did, I posted the following letter:

A CALL FOR DECORUM, COURTESY AND RESPECT

FOR EACH OTHER

Ever since I joined this group, I have watched the way members engage in conversations and how arguments are presented and challenged. I am firmly of the opinion that in a group such as this where we have people of different faiths and beliefs, there is an orderly way in which things can be done, in order that our conversations may be beneficial. For instance, the major goal of someone who advocates for his religious beliefs should be the clear presentation of such beliefs, in a manner that others can easily understand perfectly. When we read your presentations, we should be able to know the core beliefs of your religion; and see reasons that are capable of persuading us to become adherents of your belief system. This should be done with decorum, courtesy and respect.

It is sad that this has not been the case in this group. Most of what has been done so far is the unreasonable criticism and condemnation of each other's faith. I have realized that such criticisms and condemnations have been as a result of inaccurate or no understanding of what other people believe. We are quick to condemn another man's religion based on what we think they believe, which is more often than not a result of our inaccurate or insufficient knowledge about their actual beliefs.

We need to engage due diligence to research about other religions in an objective manner. Problems arise when we speak without doing proper research. It is even worse when we research with biased and preconceived notions about other religions. You are wrong if you study the holy books or other materials of another religion with the sole aim of finding reasons for criticisms and condemnation. One should engage in such research for the purpose of finding the truth, and knowing exactly what other people believe. You will never know the truth, if you are not objective and deliberately devoid of bias and unreasonable sentiments.

I do not think it is possible for you to persuade me to be-lieve in what you believe, if you lack basic manners. If you cannot present your position or communicate with courtesy and respect, then you have failed woefully from the beginning. How can you insult and condemn me and what I already believe in a condescending manner, and still expect me to believe that what you are trying to convince me about is worthy of my attention. What I see at first is your attitude, and it speaks louder than your words. Shouldn't I be skeptical that perhaps, I may become as unruly as you are, once I am converted to your religion? In fact, it is first and foremost the attitudes of people that prevent others from contemplating their religion.

In essence, your priority should be to make me understand exactly what you believe. It shouldn't be the aggressive and uninformed condemnation of what I already believe. When your manner of communication is polite and courteous, you may not need to say much before I believe your position is true.

Your attitude and respect for me speaks volumes about the propriety or otherwise of your religion.

***

You see, most times, religious crises result from misconceptions, rigidly held views and unnecessary suspicion. People with ulterior motives trigger and exploit this to their advantage, benefitting heavily from the hatred, violence and other unpleasant circumstances that emanate therefrom. It is same for tribal and political crises.

Take for instance, someone from a particular group may be moved to hate or even take up arms against people from another group, as a result of the wrong interpretation of their beliefs. Once people who create trouble are able to promote lies or misconceptions about different groups, they succeed in putting them in a position where they are at loggerheads with each other. This is exactly how wars begin.

Nigeria is diversified on many fronts. We have multiple religions, ethnicities, social persuasions, political affiliations, etc. Our diversity is such that can either be exploited for good or bad purposes. When we look at the current state of affairs in our country, it becomes obvious that our diversity has been exploited more for bad reasons. It is on account of such exploitation that we witness diverse crisis that are hinged on our differences.

The direct opposite would be the case if we deliberately exploit the advantages of our diversity, with the intent to advance our country in positive directions.

Our society is shaped by ideologies that form mindsets with which people operate. There are opinion makers behind the scene who consciously generate ideologies and skillfully transmit them into the minds of other members of the society. These opinion makers are usually a small fraction of the general populace in any given society. They are like potters, shaping clay with the use of media platforms and other forms of engagement. Most times, the masses act out their scripts unconsciously. As long as these opinion makers are able to propagate lies that form wrong opinions, the negative effects on our society will be devastating.

Young Nigerians must move to set things right along this line. It would have been convenient to say that current opinion makers should take up the responsibility of rendering our historical narratives – and other factors that affect our peaceful coexistence – with veracity. But as it stands right now, it is by the instrumentality of the schemes of past and existing opinion makers that we are where we are today. Some of them have deliberately set Nigeria on a collision course with calamity, certainly for their selfish benefits and those of their sponsors.

They do this, notwithstanding the setbacks occasioned on us and our country by their actions. This ought not to be.

Times without number, we have heard that "young people must begin to take the destiny of this country into their hands." This statement is becoming stale, owing to the fact that we hardly follow through with actions on all necessary fronts. New opinion makers who have the interest of this country at heart must emerge. To achieve this, it starts with genuine determination backed with the deliberate efforts of young Nigerians who have resolved to develop our country and advance her cause beyond its current state.

We must consciously labour to present the whole truth about our history and how it is unnecessary to sustain the current suspicion and hatred for each other. This is the only way through which we can reshape today and tomorrow in positive dimensions.

Venturing into this would definitely involve a lot of time-and-resource-consuming research, consistent enlightenment and other activities, but the end result would be worth the while. Notwithstanding the fact that it will not be an easy task, it is achievable once we have visions of the bigger picture.

We would make use of the readily available tools of social media and other platforms to permeate our society with the truth. I believe this is the start point from whence we can begin to have the kind of orientation and disposition required to tackle problems like tribalism, nepotism, blind sycophancy, violence, corruption, and other vices. Young Nigerians must arise beyond the limitations set by those who intend to keep us stuck where we are forever.

We must consistently work together to generate more measures through which we could reshape Nigeria for good.

Thereafter, we must work things out, in line with the blue-prints we are able to come up with.

If indeed we are fed up with the negative effects of magnifying our diversity to negative and dangerous proportions, we must brace up to the challenges of setting things right.

Once we can attain unity and faith, there is nothing that can stand in the way of our peace and progress.

Think about these things deeply.

Let THE CONVERSATION begin.

Yours,

Ogbole Agala.

<u>*Seventh Letter*</u>
RIGHT CHANNELS

Dear Young Nigerian,

When we speak concerning the wellbeing of our country and the protection of our collective interests, can we rightly say our opinions, desires, suggestions, recommendations, etc. – especially the constructive ones – are directed to the appropriate quarters as they ought to? When we speak, do we really speak into intended ears? When we write things like "open letters" do the persons we address such letters to ever get to read them? Or are we just satisfied with letting them out to members of the public, not minding whether or not we hit our main target? Is the social media the most effective platform to air our views on sensitive matters? When we share opinions on social media, do we do so for fun or trend's sake, to ruffle feathers, promote propaganda and unhealthy rivalry on a wider scale and in an easier way? Or we do so for the right reasons like starting healthy conversations and contributing ideas towards national development at the instance of appropriate stakeholders?

We cannot deny that from time to time, important opinions and feasible recommendations on national issues yield positive results when shared on social media platforms. However, to hold the government more accountable, we must send very strong messages to them through appropriate channels. We must deliberately and persistently go beyond all we do on social media, to ensure our opinions and recommenda-tions effectively reach appropriate quarters where they can be considered and given the life they require. And we would push further to see to it that such giving-of-life is not just talked about like mysteries by politicians or relevant stakeholders, but that they are obvious enough for everyone to see and be cleared of any reasonable doubts.

This brings to mind the functions of the legislative arm of government – the people who represent us in government, right from the grassroots up to the national level.

What exactly are the actual functions of government offi-cials such as Local Government Counselors and Members of State and National Houses of Assembly?

In this context, the word "representative" connotes an indi-vidual who acts on behalf of another individual or group of individuals. In politics, authority is delegated to representatives by the represented, and so whatever they do should be a reflection of the collective desires of majority of the people they represent. For instance, a Bill sponsored by a representative and presented before a state or national assembly should be an offshoot of elaborate consultations with the people whose interests are represented. In fact, presentations before any Assembly should be the climax of a procedure through which members of the public had aired their views and made pragmatic recommendations on topical issues that affect them, either directly or indirectly.

There is something we have been failing to do. We have not been very deliberate about putting questions directly to politicians that represent us. More often than not, we only express our grievances against politicians generally, without calling them out individually, holding them accountable and demanding to be acquainted with what they have done with the mandates we handed them. When we elect representatives into political offices, there should be this consciousness – both on our part and theirs – that they man such offices to represent our collective interests. In line with this, their actions should be tailored towards accomplishing our collective desires and aspirations that are realistic and development-driven.

A few persons hold representative positions because we all cannot do so at a time; therefore those we fix in the said positions should amplify our collective voice, by projecting what we agree upon. This is as opposed to the activities of selfish politicians, whose ears are wired to pick and listen only to voices of hungry self-seeking sycophants or fellow politicians, laced with insatiable greed and deliberate evil. With what is on ground in our contemporary political terrain, it is a lot easier for many people to view politicians as some sort of gods, rather than the servants they actually should be for real. The longer we sustain this erroneous mentality, the deeper we get plunged into the rot and uncertainties with which public offices are run today.

You see, most of the atrocities perpetrated by our leaders are consequent upon insufficient knowledge on the part of the masses. The fact that we may either be ignorant or indifferent about certain vital components of the socio-political sphere gives room for wicked politicians to enjoy prosperity in their deadly ventures.

For instance, how many of us know pretty much about the intricate politics that goes on at Local Government and State levels; especially as in-depth reports are scarcely made about such by conventional media?

As we have said before, the foremost function of each Local Government Councilor, Member of a State House of Assembly, and Member of the House of Representatives, as well as each Senator, is to convey the challenges and desires of members of their constituency to the house where they sit, ensuring that relevant legislations are made, and actions taken to address such challenges.

Representatives ought to give regular feedbacks to members of their constituencies regarding what transpired at the floor of the house, in relation to the processes they took there on account of their people.

You see, these people are meant to serve us. It is by right that we must enjoy the developments they ought to bring to our communities. Contrary to how they make it seem, they do us no favour by performing the duties they were elected to perform. We must understand these things and act accordingly, otherwise they will never see the need to imbibe accountability; and also, we may never see the need to demand it from them. We must ensure that representatives go beyond just having "honourable" in front of their names with no visible achievements in their communities to show for it. We must deliberately seek in-depth knowledge about political happenings both in our immediate and remote environments. We should know the key actors from ward councils, up to the highest political offices.

As young Nigerians, we must begin to ask questions and demand answers from those we elect to serve and represent us. We must break free from the chains of that mentality that prompts us to regard politicians as gods; they are not!!! They are our servants, and the earlier this sinks into our hearts, the better for us. If they are not useful to us and our immediate societies, we must demand for their recall, let others take their place. This is what we must do to secure guarantees of our wellbeing and that of our country.

Let me state once again that we must begin to ask politicians relevant questions and demand accurate and verifiable answers. They must know we are not all selfishly after the crumbs of ill-gotten wealth, but the overall development of our society. In addition to the advocacies we carry out on social media, we ought to push for direct interactions with those who represent us. This would be more impactful than dealing with them from a distance.

How exactly can this be done?

First, we must demand and see to it that our representatives at every level create functional avenues through which they engage members of the public (especially those they represent directly) in meaningful interactions at regular intervals. Such interactions should be aimed at working to promote common developmental goals, and not pursuant to the attainment of selfish and ungodly objectives. We should do all it takes to ensure that our representatives interact with us beyond campaign seasons when they return home with bogus words and sham projects, all in a bid to seek our votes and support for forthcoming elections. We should demand to have meetings with them face to face, and/or on specifically designated online platforms. Thereafter, recommendations from such interactions should be developed and pushed forward, until their contents are actualized.

Apart from reflecting our ideas on Bills, our representatives should also direct our meaningful views on everyday issues to appropriate authorities in the executive, judiciary and even the legislative arms of government. They ought also to ensure that our discussions addressed to particular individuals reach such individuals as, and at when due.

This is the only way through which the masses can be actively involved in governance; thereby making our representatives perform their duties effectively. If things remain otherwise, our reasonable expectations may never come to pass, as they may die untimely deaths when transmitted through wrong mediums.

Until we push towards channeling meaningful developmental ideas and opinions rightly and strategically, we may keep directing arrows off target! If this remains the case, the expected development and advancement of our country may never be actualized.

Think about these things deeply.

Let THE CONVERSATION begin.

Yours,

Ogbole Agala.

Eighth Letter

PARTICIPATION

Dear Young Nigerian,

The pages of history are replete with names and accomplishments of young Nigerians whose active political participation ensured the attainment of independence from colonial rule, and determined the shape of subsequent self-governance. Posterity will never forget those who took the bull of politics by the horns, bringing national development thereby – against all odds.

However, in contemporary times, there is a dearth of youth participation in frontline politics, owing diverse hindrances.

Other than engaging in voting exercises, frontline politics is not accessible to the average Nigerian youth. This is notwithstanding the passing of the "Not Too Young to Run" Bill, through which the ages from which political aspirants become qualified to run for offices have been reduced.

Financial constraints still remain the biggest hurdle in front of so many young Nigerians who intend to run for political offices. This is the reason why right now, most successful young politicians are either from affluent families with long political histories, or they are being supported and sponsored by affluent individuals or groups. Generally, the economic constraints affect the public support of young Nigerians in politics, making it difficult for them to match older politicians. There are also problems of cabalism and perceived insecurity. A young aspirant may be threatened by existing cabals, especially if he or she is determined to come out as a sincere politician. The institutions of the state, as well as the enormous resources at the disposal of so called established politicians may be used to clamp down the progress of young aspirants.

Another major problem lies in the fact that on account of prevailing circumstances over the years, there is this notion in the minds of many young Nigerians that politics is for the corrupt. These and many other factors limit the opportunities for youth participation in politics. As it stands at the moment, we have limited opportunities for effective participation in inclusive decision-making processes, consequent upon which we feel excluded and marginalized in our societies. Considering the enormous benefits of youth participation in politics, it is easily discernable that Nigeria is missing out on a whole lot. If national development is a key objective of the Nigerian government and all relevant stakeholders, the system at all levels must support youth participation in politics by granting access and opportunities to young people, in order that they may play key leadership roles adequately. There are various ways through which these things can be achieved.

First, there must be deliberate promotion of an enabling environment for youth participation in a broad range of processes and areas like electoral and legislative procedures, public administration and governance at local, state and national levels. This can be attained by the instrumentality of legal frameworks, policies and plans.

Also, there must be promotion of young people's skills and capacities to participate actively in democratic processes. This can be attained by the establishment of leadership training institutions and allied facilities. There should also be opportunities for youth internships in legislative houses.

Political participation should go beyond casting of votes. Young people must be involved in the entire election process, having level playing grounds with those who may be older or more affluent.

In the same vein, political enlightenment should be given to students at secondary and tertiary levels. Pending when they attain the required ages, they should be trained and made ready to participate actively in politics.

Young-people-led community development programs and volunteering organizations should also be supported by the government. Youth movements should be dealt with in a respectable way, with priority given to their voices.

All of these nonetheless, it is obvious that we cannot trust or rely on the government to do these things for us, judging by their antecedents. We must either make fervent demands that these things be done, or we get them done by ourselves, as much as it lies within our power. We cannot afford to take chances, because we know the enormous benefits inherent in effective youth participation in politics. We know that it guarantees the sprouting of fresh and innovative ideas which would guarantee national development and combat contemporary challenges. Nigeria is in dire need of such. As young people, we are more prone to exercise zeal, enthusiasm and flexibility when it comes to making decisions that are aimed at the betterment of our society. Considering the fact that the young people constitute that bulk of our gross populace, our involvement in politics will enable us frame more effective policies on issues affecting us, as opposed to older politicians who may be out of tune with contemporary realities. Furthermore, we possess the capacity to successfully engage in peace building and leading nonviolent revolutions, with the use of new technologies to mobilize our society in ways that will bring about positive change.

Now, we must be strategic in our approach towards attaining set goals. In line with this, we must understand that effective and meaningful youth political participation has any or all of three major attributes. First, it can be consultative, such that we bond together to share ideas on how to go about engaging the system in ways that will guarantee our active participation in politics, and also advance causes that would be of benefit to us and our society at large.

The second attribute entails youth-led participation, where young people have a direct impact on decision-making within their own communities. We can do this effectively because we are conversant with happenings in and around our communities. Technology plays a very vital role here, giving us an edge over the older generation. Thus, we possess the ability to properly handle and expunge undesirable circumstances if given the opportunity.

Thirdly, it can involve youth collaborative participation, where we effectively take part in regular political decision-making processes, from the grassroots up to the national level. We must give enormous support to our peers who aspire for political offices. We must do so wholeheartedly.

It is sad that at the moment, although we have lost faith in the older crop of politicians who are responsible for the ruins of Nigeria, we hardly place any faith in our peers who are capable of turning the tides. We mock our friends who aspire for political offices, drawing conclusions that they would be unable to match so called established politicians or the minions they sponsor. This is because we regard politics as a game that is usually swayed in favour of he who has more money, whether or not such a person possesses the qualities of a leader who is capable of delivering on the mandates entrusted in his hands. We fail to realize that the actual power lies in our hands, and we can effectively influence the state of affairs in our country, if we band together and pursue developmental goals with one voice. We must learn to support our peers, in order to defeat and end the reigns of those who use their affluence to plunge our country deeper into undesirable conditions. We must begin to do this deliberately, and also mobilize as many young people as possible to join us, thereby strengthening our voice and boosting our impacts.

As for our peers who aspire for political offices, you must realize that the singular fact that you are young will not guarantee our support. You must be able to show sufficiently that you have a clear vision, and that this vision is backed by your capacity to effectively man the office which you seek to occupy. You must also be devoid of the desire to pursue selfish interests in place of such interests that are for our collective good. We would not allow sentiments determine the positions to which our minds are swayed, for we would rather not support your ambition if it is laden with selfishness and obvious inclinations towards incompetence. Active participation in politics affords us the opportunity to champion the cause of a new Nigeria, one we can sincerely be proud of.

We must do these things, bearing in mind that Nigeria is ours to make, and not to mar.

Think about these things deeply.

Let THE CONVERSATION begin.

Yours,

Ogbole Agala.

<u>*Ninth Letter*</u>
JOB OPPORTUNITIES

Dear Young Nigerian,

The statement "there are no job opportunities in Nigeria…" has transformed into a kind of "school of thought" that consistently superimposes itself on the minds of many Nigerians, both young and old. It influences our thoughts and directs actions on so many fronts.

No doubt, a lot of young Nigerians are without a means of livelihood. Thus, they encounter a whole lot difficulty while trying to meet basic needs. This makes the quest for surviv-al the most paramount preoccupation in the minds of many. We can conveniently say that the strongly held view that job opportunities are lacking is hinged on the fact that a whole lot of us are unable to engage in productive ventures – especially in light of our individual or collective percep-tions about what befits our qualifications.

Now, I must say there is a very serious problem with the way we view certain things. Many of us are guilty of up-holding a stereotype that exalts white collar jobs over blue collar jobs; and this has done more harm than good to our welfare and the development of our society. Educational choices are also made along this line, as a result of the fact that society attaches more importance to certain careers, thereby influencing most of us to prioritize certain profes-sional courses over others.

Most times, we are more concerned about the perceived prestige and financial security we feel may be derived from becoming certain kinds of professionals or working in certain places. In fact, the pursuit of white collar jobs is the major reason why many persons work so hard to study specific courses and get "good degrees" so they could have an edge that is capable of granting them access into rare privileges – through narrow gates of employment. This is further amplified by the huge emphasis placed on paper qualifications, with little or no considerations for practical skills, which ought to be regarded as "actual qualification."

Many young Nigerian graduates submit all manner of applications to multinational companies, government agencies, as well as other private establishments, especially upon conclusion of the National Youth Service. Such endeavors are not necessarily bad in themselves, but considering the ways they are carried out, we could arrive at a subjective conclusion that what is at play is an extension of the colonial servitude mentality, which facilitates a disposition that regards some sort of dependence as the only means of survival. A lot of us get disappointed when our hopes are dashed, upon the realization that our dream job opportunities may just be mere components of wishful thinking. Some people end up going round cycles, wasting a lot of time repeating application processes. Others end up resorting to crime as a result of frustration, loss of hope or desperation. Our daily experiences make it easier for us to believe the statement that "there are no job opportunities."

Contrary to popular expectations, the bitter truth is that the current socio-political and socio-economic systems in place create no room to accommodate the large number of graduates flooding out of higher institutions every now and then.

While we advocate for an overhaul of the entire system to accommodate propellants of advancement that are in alignment with present-day global standards, we must do well to also face current realities the way they are right now, pending when we begin to yield the fruits of our advocacies.

Considering contemporary realities, it feels safe to say that in our clime, the main purpose of schooling should be to broaden a student's horizon, such that they are able to recognize and positively explore opportunities for personal benefits and also for the good of society at large.

Seeing the way things turn out after graduation, a lot of young Nigerians regard our entire schooling system as absolute "scam." This is because many years after their rigorous toils in school, they are unable to find suitable employments with which they can put to practice all the theories they learned while in school.

It is difficult to see what the government has done – through the system we have in place, to tackle the prevailing issue of unemployment and underemployment. However, if we keep waiting endlessly on the government, the essence of having an education in this part of the world is lost. In fact, the indifference and lack of resolve or willpower of the government, as well as the somewhat pretentious front displayed with regards to this issue is so obvious. This should propel us to think of viable alternatives that will guarantee our survival in the meantime, while we hope and work towards changing the entire system for good.

We must realize that every man has a slate on which he drafts his fortune. More often than not, the actions of politicians portray the fact that the government does not necessarily have the interests of the masses in mind when they make and implement policies.

Notwithstanding all of the foregoing, one may be tempted to ask: "what exactly do we mean whenever we talk about the government providing job opportunities?" This is because there is a gross misconception with regards to the actual meaning of "job opportunities." Many of us think about this along the lines of being employed by the government as civil servants in one ministry or another.

There is a way most Nigerian government establishments are run that leaves more to be desired. If you are faced with the unruly behaviours exhibited by many civil servants in the course of performing their duties, you will find it easy to understand exactly why it is difficult for the entire government apparatus to cause any reasonable change or guide Nigeria through a path of practical advancement.

We should not expect anything less from nonchalant and recalcitrant government workers, as many of them got there through one form of connection or another, and not on merit. They are sustained in office by the said connections; hence they are not afraid of the consequences that ought to naturally follow their misbehaviors. Expecting passion and dedication from such persons who are there only on account of the people they know – and for the sole purpose of receiving bank alerts at the end of each month, is tantamount to expecting members of a kindergarten class to engage successfully in advanced rocket science.

A careful investigation into how work is done in these state-owned offices – as well as the disposition of many public employees, makes one wonder if more civil service opportunities should be created.

In clamouring for the provision of job opportunities, more emphasis should be placed on the word "opportunities." What we should demand for is the creation of opportunities by a systematic initiation and perpetuation of enabling environments for businesses to thrive within the country. It is more reasonable to push towards getting the government to create the said enabling environments through which individuals and groups can explore their potentials independently, rather than focusing our energy on clamouring for the creation of jobs in such a narrow sense.

In a bid to drive towards the actualization of enabling environments, an inevitable step the government must take is the deliberate formulation of strategic policies that are both feasible and empirical in nature, after due consultations with relevant experts. Such policies should be focused on promoting benefits such as the availability of loans and grants, with little or no interests; tax exemptions for startup entrepreneurs – at least for the first three to five years of the commencement of their businesses, etc.

Our advocacy should be focused on this. To wait for the government alone to create actual jobs is to wait for sunlight in the middle of the night. We may wait forever.

While making the foregoing demands from the government, we must realize that the bulk of work rests upon our shoulders. As young people, we must begin think outside the box of securing certain kinds of jobs for the sake of inherent financial and other forms of security.

We must begin to look in and around our society in order to arrive at ideas which could solve problems and generate income at the same time. It is high time we start settling ourselves by ourselves, instead of going round the endless cycles of getting angry and heaping blames on the government and any "big man" around. This would also be of more benefit to us than trekking round town with old brown envelopes, worn out shoes and battered emotions. From all indications, the government does not attach a tag of fore-most priority to this part of our welfare.

In essence, it is of utmost necessity that we renew our minds and change the ways we think concerning jobs and careers, if we must improve on the wellbeing of our lives and our society at large.

We must begin to ask very reasonable questions and give objective answers to questions in this regard.

For example, what is wrong with a graduate starting up a "road side" business and growing such into a world class venture? What is wrong if the initial profit is as low as ₦10 per day? Who says we must all work in oil companies? Who says we must begin to earn so called "fat salaries" immediately? What about venturing into agriculture? What about vocational jobs like carpentry, fashion designing and other artisan activities? What stops us from picking up simple "hand dirtying" jobs and modernizing or repackaging them? It is most likely that our problem here is anchored on an erroneous sense of pride, bloated ego and many detrimental attitudes that are inconsistent with practical reality. Many of us just want to live the kind of life we see on screens, especially without working for it.

With regards to venturing into businesses, we may blame our hesitation on the absence of funds or some sort of inexplicable fear. However, if we sit back to ponder deeply, we may realize that the real problem here is not the unavailability of funds per se, but the sustenance of an erroneous mentality that despises little beginnings.

If only we could see that there are so many needs in our society clamouring for attention and solutions, we would understand that meeting such needs is like a double edged sword that serves the purpose of sustaining the society and also enhancing the livelihood of persons who solve problems. Solving problems and meeting everyday needs around us are the surest ways to clear the dark clouds over our fortunes. With persistence, there is a guarantee that we shall be set on a path that leads to financial freedom and independence, such that we are able to do more than survive, by meeting our basic needs and more. There is no guarantee that any government, white collar job or salaried employment will do this for all of us. Even if we secure such jobs, we ought to venture into other businesses, in order to have multiple streams of income. I must emphasize once again that there is no harm in venturing into entrepreneurship and picking up those so called blue collar jobs that meet needs and generate income, instead of aiming at "well-paid jobs" in big establishments, thereby missing the mark on opportunities waiting at our door steps.

We must demand that relevant stakeholders make and implement policies that promote vocational training in schools and non-conventional institutions, so as to empower young persons with requisite skills and knowledge to explore diverse opportunities. Imbibing a culture of entrepreneurship should be foremost in the contemplation of young Nigerians. Therein lays the solution to this issue of unemployment and even underemployment. Having unrealistic expectations from the government and placing total dependence on salaries are sure paths to perpetual poverty.

All we need is for the government and wealthy individuals or corporations to create the enabling environments for young Nigerians to acquire and explore vocational and entrepreneurial skills, so as to grant us the capacity to create wealth independently. Businesses should be given opportunities to thrive without unnecessary hurdles.

I have mentioned certain things the government can do. However, it is not a hidden fact that we cannot always rely on them to do what they ought to do.

We must secure the future by going the extra mile to create such opportunities for ourselves, where relevant stakeholders fail to do so. Skillful and knowledgeable young people who have attained some form of progress in their areas of specialization can give back to society by reaching out to other young persons and offering them opportunities to be trained and empowered. Doing so voluntarily sometimes is necessary, so as to ensure that financial constraints do not hinder many people from acquiring such skills.

Enlightenments and sharing of relevant information should be carried out consistently. In no time, this will help shine sufficient light on the path of those who are in the dark in several regards.

Young Nigerians can also explore the option of pooling resources together, in a bid to raise sufficient capital with which they can venture into businesses that may require huge capital for startup and maintenance. Trust should be the basis upon which the quorum of human resource is formed. Solid structures should be put in place with the help of relevant experts in these ranks, so as to avoid problems that may arise from disagreements or unforeseen circumstances. For example, young lawyers may be engaged as volunteers to carry out services that bother on the legal aspects of such ventures. Engineers within such ranks can also contribute their knowledge and skills where required.

When we adopt and apply the foregoing, we would gradually witness changes in our lives particularly, and the general outlook of our society at large.

We must think properly in this direction and leave the bandwagon of minds and mouths saying and believing the lie that there are no job opportunities in Nigeria. There are job opportunities everywhere in Nigeria, if only we could open up our eyes and see, with a resolve to follow through on the visions we are able to capture.

Think about these things deeply.

Let THE CONVERSATION begin.

Yours,

Ogbole Agala.

Tenth Letter
GIFTS

Dear Young Nigerian,

Allow me draw your attention to a very important aspect of human existence that has the capacity to make a whole lot of difference in the way our lives turn out. We really need to sit back and consider what makes people stand out in varying degrees, having divergent levels of relevance in their proximate and remote environments.

All humans cannot achieve the same things in same ways; hence, exploring individual uniqueness is very essential.

Many of us often set our gaze very far, looking in the wrong directions in search of those things that are right within or around us.

I will tell you some things about gifts/talents.

In this context, we mean those natural endowments and special abilities, on account of which a person is able to do something extraordinarily, with such ease that is uncommon to other people. More often than not, such gifts are innate, although sometimes, some people go the extra mile to learn skills that may not necessarily be part of their natural gift-ings. This goes far beyond what can be studied in line with educational curriculums provided by formal institutions.

A person may be gifted with special abilities in crafts such as: writing, singing, painting, dancing, oratory, and many other components of creativity. One way or another, every human naturally has something unique.

We must understand that although many of us may have a particular gift or talent, each person has a peculiar way he or she ought to give expression to that same gift. Just like no two humans have the same finger prints, we all have distinctive natural uniqueness.

In order to live a purposeful life on earth, there must be a deliberate search, discovery and exploration of one's gift. This is because we may never stumble accidentally upon that which is ours. After discovery, it is the extent to which a person explores his or her unique gift that they are able to stand out among men and wield such influence that is capable of making a difference in our world.

I have had some firsthand experiences along this line.

While I was in Primary school, I took my writing ability for granted. I never understood that it was worth giving some serious attention. I and some of my friends had small books in which we wrote what we called "yabs." A yab is a short verse containing somewhat funny lines with which we made jest of each other. The most creative writer – with the lines that made more people laugh, was highly respected. We had to think hard to come up with the best, so as to be on top of our game. That was my first contact with creative writing.

When I got into secondary school, I still failed to think highly of writing. This was notwithstanding the fact that I had more exposure, consequent upon which I wrote better things than yabs.

Sometimes, we may be incapable of understanding the special abilities that lie within us. This is where the guiding role of those who have gone ahead of us comes into play.

I owe a lot to my Senior Secondary English Literature teacher – Mrs. Lawal. She singled me out and gave me special attention, in spite of my recalcitrant attitude towards school in particular, and life in general. I never had any of the required literature texts, but she ensured that I participated in every class, especially drama readings. She did this by handing me texts she collected from my classmates every time we had to role-play. I participated reluctantly each time. I cannot tell how Mrs. Lawal was able to perceive my potentials at that time of my life when I had no idea about the seeds of greatness locked up on my inside. Till this day, I regard her as the first gardener who watered the particular seed that is linked to everything I have achieved, and will yet achieve through writing. She did all of these way before I began to consciously do the gardening myself. She picked me out and gave me the first dose of grooming.

It is not all young persons that may have a similar experience. Most times, you have to deliberately draw close to an older and more experienced person to groom or mentor you into discovering what is on your inside. There should be no shame about this, once you know exactly what you want.

After receiving help from those ahead of us, we must proceed to the stage where we water the seeds of our gifts by ourselves.

I had a whole new experience after secondary school. Somehow, as a result of surrounding circumstances, I realized the value of possessing a library card. I came in contact with a wide and wild array of books and assorted literature. I could not help arriving each day at the library gate by 9am – opening hours, and leaving sadly after hearing the closing bell by 4pm. I usually went home to continue with the collection of literature I had there. I realized that there is no better experience than travelling from cover to cover in the different worlds created by books. It is usually amazing, notwithstanding physical circumstances on ground.

At that point, I began to take writing seriously, ensuring that I put pen to paper every other day.

For me, writing gradually became a natural endeavor for some reasons. First, I engaged in consistent practice on a daily basis. Secondly, I learned and got addicted to the art of having my head buried in book pages for several hours every day. I lived in a whole different world altogether. You should also try this out, if you are yet to start enjoying such enormous goodness.

I had found my gift, and so I began to invest a whole lot of time, energy and resources to ensure its development and consistent improvement.

We must not stop at discovering and developing our gifts. Whenever gold is found, it remains useless if not put into use, no matter how perfectly refined it is. In the same vein, if you discover your gift and develop it to whatever level, it will be of no good if you refrain from letting it out to be of use or benefit to others and to yourself.

I had a lot of write-ups, but no one else had read them. They were only useful to me in the sense that they made me happy, but that was as far as the use went.

The year 2010 was a very significant year in my journey as a writer. I found a way to let out my works. In other words, I found a way to make my gift (and myself by extension) useful to other people. I began to submit entries for as many writing contests as I came across.

I won my first writing award in March 2010. It was a university tuition scholarship for one session. Initially, it was hard to come to terms with the fact that my work was worthy of an award. It was at that point I gained confidence in the gift I had been tending for a while. I became sure of my writing capabilities, having seen that other people found value in the things I wrote. There is a sense of fulfillment that accompanies value creation.

We must understand that no matter how good you are in whatever you do, you ought to let it out for other men to see and benefit from; otherwise your gift will be of no value.

It is very important that we understand the fact that having the right association is key. It is most unlikely that a person will succeed in isolation. You need to establish contact with people of like-mind, so as to learn more, grow and expand your access to opportunities.

Also, the number of people you influence with your gift is a very important factor in determining the extent of your success. You cannot afford to be useful to yourself alone.

Other than studying on my own, I began to join Literary Associations. I made new friends with like-minds, and had more access to opportunities.

In order to improve and gain more exposure, I took up challenges by entering for new writing contests that were way bigger than the ones in which I had participated in the past. The second writing award I got was for my entry in a state poetry contest. Besides the accolades I acquired, I gained access to the government house for the first time, where I met with people I had only seen on television before then. Indeed, a man's gift makes room for him, and brings him before great men. [Proverbs 18:16]. I have enjoyed the fulfillment of this portion of the Holy Bible first hand, on countless occasions.

After that second award, I won a third one; this time, a national essay contest. Thereafter, I received an award from the World Bank, on account of my entry for an international essay contest. I went ahead to win awards for several short-story contests.

For each of these awards, I got some cash and other rewards in addition to some beautiful plaques and other honors.

I got to understand perfectly that the pen was a very useful tool in my hands.

The circumstances surrounding one more award [other than those I have mentioned above] are most relevant to what I have been saying concerning the heights to which your gift can take you if put into proper use.

While I was in my final year at the university, I got a strange call one evening. The man on the other end of the line told me I had been nominated with two other persons as winner of a national inter-universities essay contest. He told me they had sent two invitation letters to my email address, one for me, and the other for my vice chancellor. I was invited to receive an award for my essay, while my vice chancellor was invited to receive an award on behalf of the school – on my account. When he dropped the call, I tried hard to remember the particular essay contest he talked about – I had submitted countless entries for diverse contests. Finally, I recalled it was a national contest for which I had submitted an entry two years earlier.

After printing the invitation letters from my email address, I packaged that which was meant for my Vice Chancellor and headed for her office. The protocol I had to observe and questions I answered were irritating. I was tossed here and there from one secretary to another. I cannot tell what they were thinking, but I was sure I was being maltreated.

I ended up dropping the letter with one of those officials without setting my eyes on the vice chancellor. The award ceremony was to hold in the Federal Capital Territory about two weeks from that time. I went on with my usual activities, patiently waiting for the D-day.

I got no call from the school authorities until a day to the ceremony, at a time when I was already on a bus headed to the Federal Capital Territory. I sent a message through their messenger, informing them I was already on my way to the Federal Capital Territory in preparation for the next day's award ceremony. Apparently, they had suddenly realized the essence of the letter I submitted earlier.

On the day of the ceremony, I woke up early, dressed properly and headed to the venue. I was amazed by the local and international dignitaries in attendance. It seemed like a dream. My Deputy Vice Chancellor sat on the high table. I got to know him for the first time that day. He was given a plaque for my school. In addition to my plaque, I returned home with an amount of cash that had a good number of zeros. That money was so useful at that time in ways I am unable to describe.

When I returned to school, I had express access to the Deputy Vice Chancellor's office at any time. He was highly honoured at the award ceremony and we became friends. I could tell he was so proud of me from the stories he told whenever he introduced me to his colleagues.

On a certain day when I met with him in his office, he took me to the Vice Chancellor's office. That day, I realized there was a special passage for exclusive use by the Vice Chancellor and very special guests.

We met the Vice Chancellor outside her office, and after talking with her for a while, we all walked in through that special passage. I gained express entry into that office for the first time, without the stress of going through diverse rooms and giving long explanations at several tables – to no avail. It was as if I became a celebrity of some sort, and professors – whose faces I had only seen in pictures before then, requested to take pictures with me. This may sound funny right now, but it was a very big deal back then. I really felt honoured indeed.

What was the difference between the day I met with the Vice Chancellor and the other days I tried in vain to deliver a letter to her in person? They had realized my worth, on account of the honour I brought upon the school. I bye-passed rigid protocols, because of the value I had obtained from putting my gift into use.

I have written these things for the sole purpose of encouraging you, and opening your eyes to some realities you could benefit from.

These and much more could be your experience, if you apply the steps I have explained in the course of telling my story. Do not forget that no matter who you are and where you are from; no matter the ugly circumstances that surround your existence, you can always stand out by giving expression to the gifts that are yours naturally. You could also learn and master a skill and work hard and smart to stand out in what you do. This is how to reach out and be an effective blessing to the world. Returns will always come if you remain diligent and persistent in doing what you do.

Your gift is capable of opening unimaginable doors, if only you discover, groom and let it out.

Start today.

Think about these things deeply.

Let THE CONVERSATION begin.

Yours,

Ogbole Agala.

Dear Young Nigerian,

Let THE CONVERSATION begin along these lines and many more we may generate, in the course of time.

About the Book

DEAR YOUNG NIGERIAN: THE AWAKENING is a collection of ten letters written to young Nigerians as a wakeup call. In these letters, the author expounds separate but interwoven issues about Nigeria, in a bid to inspire new conversations that will birth progressive, solution-driven actions.

DYN:TA shall inspire young Nigerians to disturb the peace of stale and undesirable status quo, till our country is set on a progressive trajectory that facilitates growth and development, through the promotion of her citizens' interests.

About the Author

Ogbole Agala is a dynamic Legal Practitioner, Advocacy Consultant, Public Speaker and Social Commentator. He is a multiple award winning author, who engages the use of his prolific writing and oratory skills to advocate diverse just and noble causes.

www.ingramcontent.com/pod-product-compliance
Lightning Source LLC
Chambersburg PA
CBHW030356280726
48655CB00019B/1917